Lightning Lessons

Instant Units

Nonfiction

Author: Teresa Domnauer
Editor: Elizabeth Goodwin

Frank Schaffer Publications®

Send all inquiries to:
Frank Schaffer Publications
8720 Orion Place
Columbus, Ohio 43240-2111

Lightning Lessons: Instant Units-Nonfiction—grades 1-2

ISBN: 0-7682-3891-9

1 2 3 4 5 6 7 8 9 10 POH 12 11 10 09 08 07

Table of Contents

Published by Frank Schaffer Publications. Copyright protected.   0-7682-3891-9 *Lightning Lessons: Nonfiction*

Introduction to Lightning Lessons

Welcome to *Lightning Lessons: Instant Units*. This unit is a self-contained, standards-based unit that presents fun, imaginative activities that will support your instruction of nonfiction reading. In this unit, students will read, analyze, discuss, and write about nonfiction books. Students will also study important vocabulary words and proper punctuation techniques.

The activities are fun and do not require hours of preparation. However, they focus in depth on the study of nonfiction reading materials. In the *Connecting With Resources* section, you will find instructions and ideas for using the reproducible pages contained in this book and the companion *Punctuation Rules* poster. Icons clearly indicate which pages are for teachers and which are for students.

You may wish to try all the activities and projects over the course of a few weeks or months, or just choose your favorites for a shorter unit. The activities in this book are designed to be flexible so that you can use them during the entire school year. Whether you do a unit of study on apples, simple machines, Africa, bears, or the human body, you can use these activities with any nonfiction books that you choose.

This unit provides teachers with flexible activities that can be adapted to a wide variety of skill levels. An assessment rubric is included to help you keep track of students' progress.

Getting Started
Introducing the Lightning Unit to Your Students

Discussion Starter
(critical thinking, comparing, describing, brainstorming)

Begin your nonfiction unit by asking your students if they know what *nonfiction* means. Write their responses on chart paper. Discuss the meaning of the word *nonfiction* and the difference between nonfiction and fiction.

KWL Chart and Reproducible
(brainstorming, describing, listening, recalling, using a graphic organizer)

Choose a nonfiction book to read your class. Refer to *Suggested Nonfiction Books* on page 5 or select a title that coordinates with a topic that your class is already studying.

Before reading the book aloud to your class, display a Know, Want to Know, Learned (KWL) chart. Invite students to share what they already know about the topic, and write their responses in the "K" part of the chart. Then, have students describe the things that they want to know about the topic. Write their questions in the "W" section of the chart. After reading the nonfiction book and studying the topic further, invite students to help you complete the "L" section of the chart, which tells what they learned.

After you have modeled several times how to fill in the KWL chart, students can do the same thing on their own. The reproducible version of the chart on page 26 can be used for any topic that your class studies.

Unit Folders
(organizing materials)

Supply each student with a manila folder to use for the unit. Throughout the unit, allow students time to decorate their folders with images related to nonfiction topics, such as animals, sports, nature, geography, etc. Students will store their journal pages, *Lightning Words*, and other resources in the folder.

Sharing
(using listening and speaking strategies)

Make sure to allow time for students to share their journal entries, other written pieces, and artwork with the whole group, a small group, or a partner. This will help students to develop their verbal communication and listening skills.

Reading Corner
(reading independently)

Set up a cozy reading corner in your classroom. Supply the corner with a variety of nonfiction books and comfortable pillows. Display student writing assignments and art projects from the unit on the walls where students can sit quietly and enjoy them.

Published by Frank Schaffer Publications. Copyright protected.　　　　0-7682-3891-9 *Lightning Lessons: Nonfiction*

Getting Started

Introducing the Lightning Unit to Your Students

Suggested Nonfiction Books

The following list is just a sample of quality nonfiction books. Look for other titles by these authors.

- *Almost Gone: The World's Rarest Animals* by Steve Jenkins
- *Arctic Tundra: Land with No Trees* by Allan Fowler (Allan Fowler has many other easy-to-read nonfiction books in the *Rookie Read-About Science* series published by Children's Press. These titles are suitable for guided reading sessions.)
- *Extreme Readers: The Bizarre Body* by Katharine Kenah
- *Carrots* by Gail Saunders-Smith
- *Feel the Wind* by Arthur Dorros
- *Ice Cream: The Full Scoop* by Gail Gibbons
- *Lithgow Palooza Readers: Drop, Drip, an Underwater Trip* by Susan Blackaby
- *A Picture Book of Benjamin Franklin* by David A. Adler (Adler has authored other biographies in this series including titles about Patrick Henry, Harriet Beecher Stowe, Sacagawea, Amelia Earhart, and many more.)
- *The Piñata Maker* by George Ancona
- *The Right Dog for the Job: Ira's Path from Service Dog to Guide Dog* by Dorothy Hinshaw Patent
- *When Marian Sang* (a biography of opera singer Marian Anderson) by Pam Muñoz Ryan

These Web sites list award-winning nonfiction books:

- http://www.ncte.org/elem/awards/orbispictus
  The National Council of Teachers of English (NCTE) Orbis Pictus Award
- http://www.ala.org/ala/alsc/awardsscholarships/literaryawds/sibertmedal/sibert_current/sibertmedalcurrent.htm
  The Robert F. Sibert Information Book Medal established by the Association for Library Service to Children (ALSC), which is a division of the American Library Association (ALA)
- http://www.childrensbookguild.org/awardnonfiction.htm
  The Children's Book Guild's nonfiction award for authors and illustrators

You should also consult your school and local children's librarians to help you choose the best informational books for each unit that your class studies.

0-7682-3891-9 *Lightning Lessons: Nonfiction*

Lightning Resources
Connecting With Resources

Lightning Words
(understanding vocabulary)

The *Lightning Words* on page 8 are vocabulary words specific to the unit. You may wish to review the meaning of one word each day during the unit. Copy the page for students to keep in their unit folders for reference.

Using the Punctuation Rules Poster
(practicing and applying punctuation rules)

This unit includes a punctuation rules poster that you can laminate and re-use throughout the unit and the school year. Review one section of the poster with your class each week or two. Read the information in the box, and go over the examples on the poster. Then, on chart paper, model how to write sentences using that specific type of punctuation.

After reading a nonfiction book to the class, write several sentences from the book on chart paper, omitting the punctuation. Invite students to help you add the correct punctuation. Additionally, students can practice writing and punctuating different types of sentences in their journals. Each time you revisit the poster, do a cumulative review of the punctuation rules that you have already covered.

Hang the poster at the front of the room, or somewhere students can easily see it. These rules will help them as they write book reports and journal entries about nonfiction books, and when they write for any subject area.

Fact and Opinion Reproducibles
(using skills and strategies of reading, understanding facts and opinions, reading comprehension)

The worksheets on pages 13–18 support instruction of the differences between fact and opinion. These worksheets are best used at the beginning of the unit when you are first introducing the concept of nonfiction to your students. The worksheets also build reading comprehension skills, and can be used for that purpose at any time during the unit.

Punctuation Activities
(practicing punctuation rules)

After several weeks of studying the punctuation poster, make copies of the punctuation activities on pages 18–25 for students to complete. The activities offer students practice using periods, question marks, exclamation points, and commas.

My Research Notes Reproducible
(researching, using sources to gather information, using vocabulary, critical thinking)

My Research Notes reproducible on page 27 will help your students learn the proper techniques for gathering and organizing information for reports. Students can use this reproducible for any subject. You can model proper note taking for your students by transferring the information from the reproducible onto chart paper. Take notes on the chart paper as you read aloud to the class from a nonfiction book.

0-7682-3891-9 *Lightning Lessons: Nonfiction*

Lightning Resources
Connecting With Resources, (cont.)

Nonfiction Book Web, My Book Report, and Biography Page
(using skills and strategies of reading, reading comprehension, using skills and strategies of writing, using a graphic organizer, using vocabulary)

On pages 28–30, you will find three different reproducible activities for students to use with nonfiction books: a nonfiction book web, a book report page, and a biography page. You may wish to model each of these activities for students. Transfer the information on each page to a sheet of chart paper. Then, after reading a nonfiction selection, invite students to help you complete one of the pages.

For the nonfiction book web, fill in the topic in the center oval. Then, in each square write related facts and details from the book about the topic. Students can try the activity on their own during your next language arts lesson. If you have emerging writers in your class, they can draw pictures or write words rather than sentences inside the boxes.

For the book report page, fill in the title, author, and illustrator. Invite students to explain the main idea of the book as you complete the "This book was about…" section. Encourage students to recall things they learned from the book and write their responses in the next section.

When assigning a book report, encourage students to take notes as they read. Refer back to the instructions for using the *My Research Notes* reproducible. Remind students not to copy sentences directly from the book and to phrase things in their own words. You can also invite students to do drawings to accompany their reports.

After reading a biography to your class, model how to use the biography page in the same way. On this page, students can include a small drawing or portrait of the person about whom they read.

0-7682-3891-9 *Lightning Lessons: Nonfiction*

Lightning Resources

Name _____

Lightning Words

Date _____

author {AW-ther} the writer of a book, play, story, or other written work

biography {BYE-AH-gruh-fee} the written story of someone's life

comma {KOM-ma} a punctuation mark that is used to separate words or phrases in a sentence

exclamation point {EX-kla-MAY-shun poynt} a punctuation mark that is used at the end of a sentence to show surprise or strong feelings

fact {FAKT} something that is known to be true

fiction {FIK-shun} writing that is made up by the author from his or her imagination

nonfiction {non-FIK-shun} writing that contains facts rather than imagined ideas

opinion {oh-PIN-yun} what someone thinks about something or somebody based on his or her own feelings, not necessarily facts

period {PEER-e-id} a punctuation mark that is used at the end of a sentence that tells something or gives a command

question mark {KWEST-shun mark} a punctuation mark that is used at the end of a sentence that asks something

title {TYE-tul} what a story is called or named

Abraham Lincoln

A. Lincoln

0-7682-3891-9 *Lightning Lessons: Nonfiction*

Lightning Connections
Connecting With Technology

(using technology, researching)

There are many Web sites you can access that are related to nonfiction:

- http://www.nationalgeographic.com/xpeditions/lessons/gk2.html

  Lessons plans from National Geographic include a variety of topics such as the Middle East, insects, the Mayflower, and much more.

- http://www.smithsonianeducation.org/students/

  The Smithsonian Institution's student site includes pages and activities on art; history and culture; science and nature; and people and places. It also has educational activity sheets for children and many areas to explore.

- http://ology.amnh.org/mythiccreatures/?src=h_nc

  The American Museum of Natural History's "Ology" section presents a variety of science topics that kids can explore, such as paleontology and astronomy.

- http://www.moma.org/destination/#

  Students can visit the Museum of Modern Art through the *Destination Modern Art* section of the museum's Web site.

- http://www.readwritethink.org/lessons/lesson_view.asp?id=183

  Adventures in Nonfiction: A Guided Inquiry Journey features detailed lesson plans and links for studying nonfiction books.

- http://www.readingrockets.org/books/interviews

  The Reading Rockets Web site includes video interviews of children's book authors, many of whom write nonfiction, such as Joanna Cole, David Adler, Seymour Simon, and Gail Gibbons.

- http://www.readwritethink.org/lessons/lesson_view.asp?id=781

  Diagram It! Identifying, Comparing, and Writing About Nonfiction Texts is a complete classroom lesson about nonfiction reading.

- http://www.gailgibbons.com

  Author Gail Gibbons' Web site includes a downloadable teaching guide that coordinates with her books. Her site also features information about her and activities for students.

To incorporate technology into your unit you can also:

- Post students' book reports, biography pages, and artwork to your school's Web site.

- Invite students to use computer software to publish their book reports and biography pages.

- Use the computer to publish a book of the class's written pieces about the nonfiction books they read.

- Construct a PowerPoint presentation of things that your class has learned while reading nonfiction books.

- Invite students to research online biographies of various people that they have read about or would like to know more about.

0-7682-3891-9 *Lightning Lessons: Nonfiction*

Lightning Connections
Connecting With Arts and Literature

(painting, drawing, brainstorming, observing, note taking, using listening and speaking strategies)

- Supply students with large sheets of construction paper so that they can create collages related to the nonfiction books they are reading. They may wish to use old magazines, crayons, markers, paint, and found objects that can be glued onto the paper.

- As an alternative to book reports on nonfiction titles, have students give oral reports. Students can write important facts on index cards and share them with the class. Students can also create posters using crayons, markers, or paint and display them as they read their oral reports.

- Have students paint a class mural about the topic you are studying. If you are studying a biography, the mural could be a timeline featuring important events in the person's life.

- Invite a professional related to the topic your class is studying, such as a doctor, an author, a sports figure, or an artist, to visit your classroom. Some parents of your students may qualify!

- For the study of biographies, have students use pastels and large construction paper to draw giant portraits of the person about whom they are reading.

- Take a field trip to a site that is related to the nonfiction topic about which your class is learning. Examples include: a factory, a museum, a sporting event, a nature sanctuary, a government building, or a music or dance performance.

- Have students write songs, poems, or fictional stories related to the nonfiction books they have read. These works of writing can be compiled into a class book.

- Have students work in small groups to write simple skits about a nonfiction book. Students can create simple costumes and props using paper bags, scraps of fabric, and found objects.

- Pair works of fiction with the nonfiction books that you read to your class. Facilitate a class discussion that relates and compares the two books.

- Invite students to do further research on a topic by using the Internet, the library, or by interviewing people.

- Dioramas are another fun project that students can do to show what they've learned about a particular topic. Students can use shoeboxes and found materials. Allow students time to share their creations with small groups or the entire class.

0-7682-3891-9 *Lightning Lessons: Nonfiction*

Lightning Connections
Connecting With Writing

(using the skills and strategies of writing, using vocabulary, critical thinking, creative thinking)

Writing Response: Student Journals
Make copies of the *My Nonfiction Journal* sheet on page 12. These sheets can be used for student journal entries throughout the unit. Students can keep their journal entries in their unit folders.

Writing Activities for Journals
The following writing excercises can help students reflect on the books that you have read to them in class. Students can also include illustrations in each of their journal entries.

- *Imagine that you are a caterpillar (or any other insect or animal that your class is studying). Describe what life is like from your point of view.*

- *Write three things that you learned from the nonfiction book read aloud in class today.*

- *Write three questions that you have about the topic covered in the nonfiction book read aloud in class today.*

- *Write about three ways that you could learn more about: (the topic your class is currently studying).*

- *For a biography that you have read: Write three events from this person's life in the order that they happened.*

- *For a biography that you have read: Write three questions that you would like to ask this person.*

- *Imagine that someone is writing a biography about you. Write three things you would want him or her to write about you.*

Lightning Activities

My Nonfiction Journal

Name _____

Date _____

Published by Frank Schaffer Publications. Copyright protected.

Lightning Activities

Name _____

Date _____

Fact and Opinion: Firefighters

(identifying facts and opinions, reading comprehension)

Read the story.

A firefighter's job is to put out fires. This can be a dangerous job. At times firefighters must go into burning houses. Sometimes they must get people out safely.

Whenever the bell rings, the firefighters rush to their trucks. They wear special boots, hats, and coats to help keep them safe from the fire.

Write an **F** if the sentence is a **fact**. A fact is something that can be proved. Write an **O** if the sentence is an **opinion**. An opinion is what someone believes or thinks.

1. _____ A firefighter's job is to put out fires.

2. _____ A firefighter's job is scary.

3. _____ Firefighters wear special clothes to help keep them safe.

4. _____ I would not want to be a firefighter.

5. _____ Firefighters rush to their trucks when the bell rings.

6. _____ Firefighters must go into burning houses.

7. _____ Being a firefighter is the best job in the world.

0-7682-3891-9 *Lightning Lessons: Nonfiction*

Lightning Activities

Name _____

Fact and Opinion: Penguins

Date _____

(identifying facts and opinions, reading comprehension, using a chart)

Read the story.

A penguin is a bird that cannot fly. Its wings look and act like flippers. Penguins are very good swimmers and spend a lot of time in the water. White belly feathers and short black feathers on their backs make them hard to see in the water. They waddle when they walk. Most wild penguins live in the southern part of the world.

Female penguins lay one to three eggs. The male penguin carries the eggs on his feet and covers the eggs with his body to keep them warm. A baby penguin is called a chick. Penguins can live up to 20 years.

1. Fill in the chart with **facts** about penguins.

Penguin Facts

How penguins travel:	
Where penguins live:	
How many eggs penguins lay:	
Name of a baby penguin:	
How long penguins live:	

2. How do you feel about penguins? Write a sentence that states your **opinion**. Then, write another sentence that tells why you feel that way.

_____

_____

0-7682-3891-9 *Lightning Lessons: Nonfiction*

Lightning Activities

Name _____

Fact and Opinion: Arctic Land

Date _____

(identifying facts and opinions, reading comprehension)

Read the passage. Then, answer the questions.

The Arctic is a place where it is very cold. The ground is covered in snow and ice most of the year. It is so cold that the breath of a person will freeze. Sometimes, the sun never shines. It stays dark during the night and day. At other times, the sun never sets. The sun shines for 24 hours.

Many animals, such as polar bears, live in the Arctic. These animals have white fur to help them look like the land they live on. It is hard to see them because they blend in with the color of the snow. Their fur is thick to help them stay warm. Some animals live in the cold ocean water. They have a thick layer of fat that keeps them warm when they swim.

1. How does a polar bear stay safe in the Arctic?

_____

_____

2. Write one fact that you learned about the Arctic.

_____

_____

3. Why did the author write this passage?
   A. to tell you about life in the Arctic
   B. to give you goose bumps
   C. to get you to visit the Arctic

4. Where might you read this passage?
   A. in a comic book
   B. in a nature magazine
   C. in a dictionary

15

Lightning Activities

Name _____

Fact and Opinion: Elephants

Date _____

(identifying and understanding facts and opinions, reading comprehension)

Read the passage. Then, answer the questions on the next page.

Have you ever looked closely at an elephant? They have some body parts that look strange. Have you ever wondered why elephants have these parts? Well, they help the elephants do things.

One of the first parts you might notice is the trunk. The trunk has many uses. It is like a nose and helps the elephant smell. It also helps an elephant grab food that is high up in trees and low on the ground.

Did you know that elephants like to swim? They can swim for hours under the water. This helps them cool off. An elephant will stick its trunk above water to get air to breathe. You might think it is a periscope, but it is just an elephant.

You might also notice how big the elephant's ears are. Have you ever wondered why they are so big? The ears help the elephant stay cool on a hot day. There are many tubes in the ear that are filled with blood. When the elephant flaps its ears, the blood is cooled. The cooled blood moves to all parts of the elephant's body to help it get cool. Now isn't that cool?

0-7682-3891-9 *Lightning Lessons: Nonfiction*

Lightning Activities

Name _____

Fact and Opinion: Elephants (cont.)

Date _____

Answer the questions below.

1. Is the story true or make-believe? How do you know this?

_____

_____

2. Write one fact you learned about elephants.

_____

_____

3. Why did the author write this passage?
   A. to get you to visit a zoo
   B. to tell how elephants swim
   C. to tell facts about an elephant's body

4. What else might the author write about?
   A. how an elephant uses its tail to hit flies
   B. where elephants live
   C. how to keep elephants safe

5. Which sentence could be added to the passage?
   A. "I flap my big ears to cool myself off."
   B. These interesting body parts all serve a purpose.
   C. The elephant flapped its ears back and forth and started to lift off the ground.

0-7682-3891-9 *Lightning Lessons: Nonfiction*

Lightning Activities

Name _____

Capital Letters and Periods

Date _____

(understanding punctuation basics, using proper punctuation)

A **statement** is a sentence that tells about something. It begins with a capital letter and ends with a period.

Examples:

We went to a magic show.

The magician was very good.

Read the examples below. Rewrite each one using capital letters and periods in the right way.

1. mel and I want to study magic _____

2. the magician made a dollar bill disappear _____

3. mel said the dollar was in his pocket _____

4. then the magician pulled it from his ear_____

5. next he threw plates into the air _____

6. they didn't disappear _____

7. but they landed on the floor and did not break _____

8. i want to be a good magician_____

Try This: Write two statements about what you want to do when you grow up.

0-7682-3891-9 *Lightning Lessons: Nonfiction*

Lightning Activities

Name _____

That's the Point

Date _____

(discriminating types of sentences, using proper punctuation)

A **period** (.) is used at the end of a sentence that tells something or gives a command.

Read the sentences. Put a period at the end of each sentence that tells something or gives a command.

Examples: **Telling Sentence:** I am happy.
Command: Please do your homework.

1. Please sit down

2. John is tired

3. Did you see your sister

4. Eat your dinner

5. Why is Taylor running

6. That mouse ate all the cheese

7. My friends sang a birthday song

8. I like dinosaurs

9. Please answer the telephone

10. Are you hungry

0-7682-3891-9 *Lightning Lessons: Nonfiction*

Lightning Activities

Name _____

Questions

Date _____

(discriminating types of sentences, using proper punctuation)

A **question** is a statement that asks something. It begins with a capital letter and ends with a question mark.

Rewrite each example below to make it into a question. Then, answer the question.

1. where do you go to school

    _____

2. how old are you

    _____

3. what is your favorite subject in school

    _____

4. what is your favorite activity outside school

    _____

5. do you have any pets

    _____

6. who is your favorite person

    _____

Try This: Think of other things about you. What questions could you ask like the ones above?

20

Published by Frank Schaffer Publications. Copyright protected.

Lightning Activities

What's the Question?

Name _____

Date _____

(discriminating types of sentences, using proper punctuation)

Think of a question to go with each answer. Remember to use a question mark.

1. Question: _____

   _____

   Answer: An apple is red.

2. Question: _____

   _____

   Answer: Birds fly south in winter.

3. Question: _____

   _____

   Answer: Cats climb trees.

4. Question: _____

   _____

   Answer: Horses eat grass.

0-7682-3891-9 *Lightning Lessons: Nonfiction*

Lightning Activities

Name _____

What a Surprise!

Date _____

(discriminating types of sentences, using proper punctuation)

Use an **exclamation point** (!) to show surprise or strong feelings.

Read each sentence. Ask yourself if it shows surprise or strong feelings. If it does, put an exclamation point at the end.

1. I can't believe we won

2. Oh, no

3. It's very cold today

4. Wow, I can't believe it

5. Hooray

6. Watch out

7. This sweater is warm

8. I don't like that book

9. Be careful

10. Ouch

0-7682-3891-9 *Lightning Lessons: Nonfiction*

Lightning Activities

Name _____

Date _____

Punctuation Zoo

(discriminating types of sentences, using proper punctuation)

Read the story. Put a period after a telling sentence. Put a question mark after an asking sentence. Put an exclamation point after an excited sentence.

1. We went to the zoo___

2. We saw the lions___

3. Have you seen lions___

4. Wow, do they have big teeth___

5. We saw the monkeys___

6. Do you think monkeys are funny___

7. Do you like the elephants___

8. I rode an elephant___

9. Then we went home___

10. What a great day___

23

0-7682-3891-9 *Lightning Lessons: Nonfiction*

Lightning Activities

Name _____

Statements, Questions, and Exclamations

Date _____

(critical thinking, comprehension, discriminating types of sentences, using proper punctuation)

Add a period, question mark, or exclamation point to each sentence.

1. I found twenty dollars at the park yesterday

2. I have to clean my room

3. Where did Mom put my soccer ball

4. I met a movie star in the grocery store

5. Have you seen my skateboard

6. Don't go near that snake

Write one statement, one question, and one exclamation below. Be sure to use the correct punctuation.

1. Statement: _____

    _____

2. Question: _____

    _____

3. Exclamation: _____

    _____

24

Lightning Activities

Name _____

Using Commas

Date _____

(critical thinking, comprehension, using commas in a series)

Use a comma in a series of three or more persons or things.

Examples: Melissa has roses, pansies, and daisies in her garden.
Tommy, Gary, Adam, and Jerry are my best friends.

Add commas where they are needed in each sentence.

1. I have a dog a cat and a bird at home.

2. I brought an apple a sandwich and a cookie for lunch.

3. Do you want to go to the zoo the park or the movies today?

4. This book is about Jesse Owens' life career and trip to the Olympics.

5. Would you like to eat an apple a banana or a carrot?

25

 0-7682-3891-9 *Lightning Lessons: Nonfiction*

Lightning Activities

Name _____

KWL Chart

Date _____

(assessing knowledge, brainstorming, critical thinking, reading comprehension, using a graphic organizer)

Topic: _____

What I **K**now:
What I Want to Know:
What I Learned:

0-7682-3891-9 *Lightning Lessons: Nonfiction*

Lightning Activities

Name _____

My Research Notes

Date _____

(using sources to gather information, using vocabulary, critical thinking)

Tips for taking notes:

- Make sure the source you use is related to the subject you are researching.
- Write your notes using your own words. It is best not to copy word-for-word from your source.
- When you are done, review your notes.
- Check to see if you have all the information you need.

Type of source: _____

Title of source: _____

Subject I am researching: _____

Fact 1: _____ Page (s): _____

_____

_____

Fact 2: _____ Page (s): _____

_____

_____

Fact 3: _____ Page (s): _____

_____

_____

0-7682-3891-9 *Lightning Lessons: Nonfiction*

Lightning Activities

Nonfiction Book Web

Name _____

Date _____

(comprehension, recalling details, using a graphic organizer)

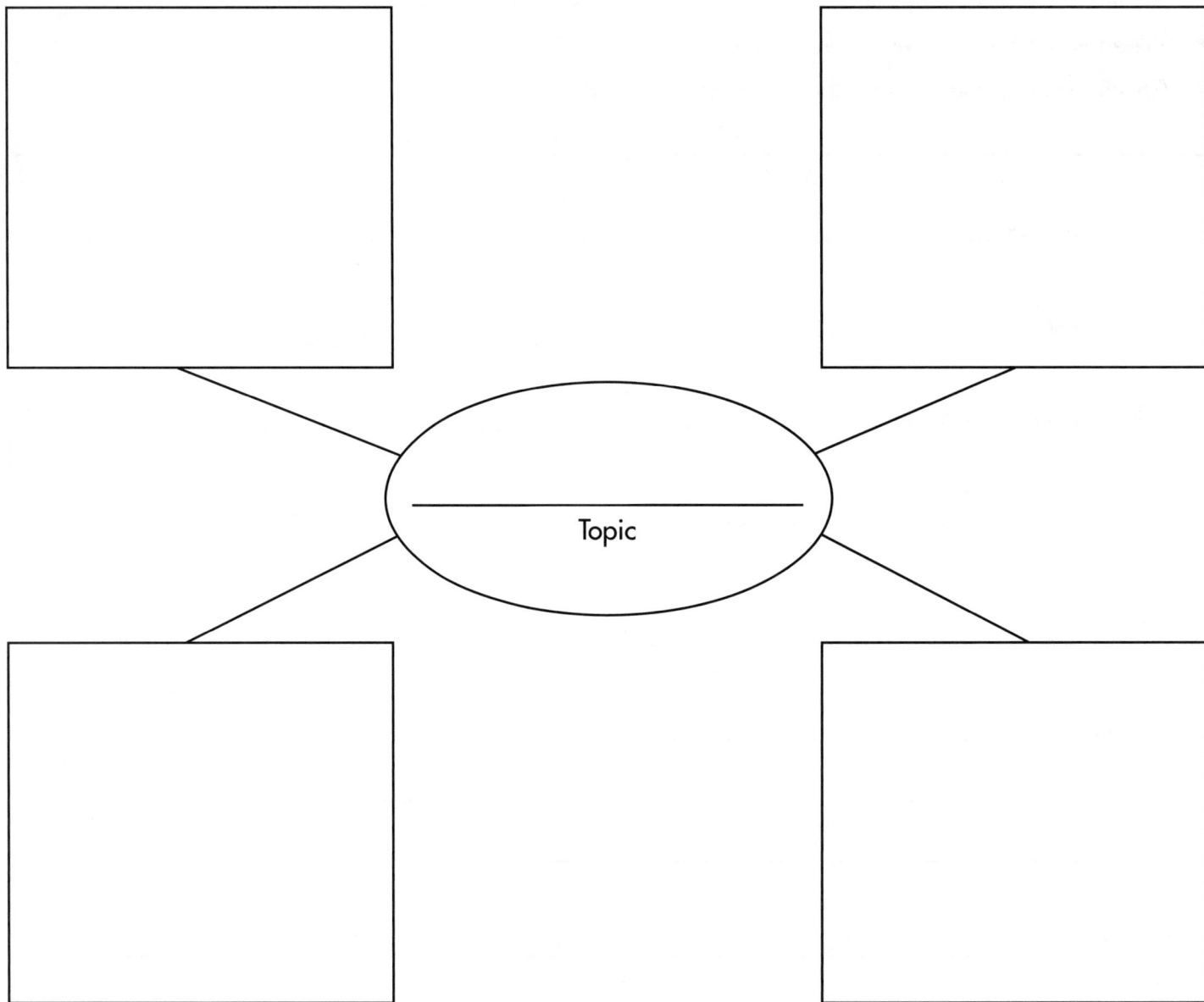

Topic

0-7682-3891-9 *Lightning Lessons: Nonfiction*

Lightning Activities

Name _____

My Book Report

Date _____

(reading comprehension, using the skills and strategies of writing, using vocabulary)

Title of book:_____

Author: _____ Illustrator:_____

This book was about: _____

_____

_____

_____

Three things that I learned:

1. _____

_____

2. _____

_____

3. _____

_____

0-7682-3891-9 *Lightning Lessons: Nonfiction*

Lightning Activities

Biography Page

Name _____

Date _____

(reading comprehension, using the skills and strategies of writing, using vocabulary)

Title of book:_____

Author: _____ Illustrator:_____

This book was about: _____

Date of birth: _____ Date person died:_____

Important things this person did: _____

_____

_____

_____

_____

_____

0-7682-3891-9 *Lightning Lessons: Nonfiction*

Lightning Assessment

Answer Key

Page 13

1. F	3. F	5. F
2. O	4. O	6. F
		7. O

Page 14

1. How penguins travel: they swim or walk
   Where penguins live: southern part of the world
   How many eggs penguins lay: one to three
   Name of a baby penguin: chick
   How long penguins live: up to 20 years

2. Answers will vary.

Page 15

1. The polar bear's fur makes it hard to see them on the white snow and ice.
2. Answers will vary.
3. A
4. B

Page 17

1. The story is true because it gives information about elephants.
2. Answers will vary.
3. C
4. A
5. B

Page 18

1. Mel and I want to study magic.
2. The magician made a dollar bill disappear.
3. Mel said the dollar was in his pocket.
4. Then the magician pulled it from his ear.
5. Next he threw plates into the air.
6. They didn't disappear.
7. But they landed on the floor and did not break.
8. I want to be a good magician.

Page 19

1. .		7. .
2. .		8. .
4. .		9. .
6. .		

Page 20

1. Where do you go to school?
2. How old are you?
3. What is your favorite subject in school?
4. What is your favorite activity outside school?
5. Do you have any pets?
6. Who is your favorite person?

Page 21

1. What color is an apple? or What fruit is red?
2. Where do birds fly in winter? or When do birds fly south?
3. What do cats climb? or What climbs trees?
4. What do horses eat? or What eats grass?

Page 22

1. I can't believe we won!	6. Watch out!
2. Oh, no!	9. Be careful!
4. Wow, I can't believe it!	10. Ouch!
5. Hooray!	

Page 23

1. .	4. !	7. ?
2. .	5. .	8. . or !
3. ?	6. ?	9. .
		10. !

Page 24

1. I found twenty dollars at the park yesterday!
2. I have to clean my room.
3. Where did Mom put my soccer ball?
4. I met a movie star in the grocery store!
5. Have you seen my skateboard?
6. Don't go near that snake!

Answers will vary.

Page 25

1. I have a dog, a cat, and a bird at home.
2. I brought an apple, a sandwich, and a cookie for lunch.
3. Do you want to go to the zoo, the park, or the movies today?
4. This book is about Jesse Owens' life, career, and trip to the Olympics.
5. Would you like to eat an apple, a banana, or a carrot?

0-7682-3891-9 *Lightning Lessons: Nonfiction*

Lightning Assessment

Nonfiction Unit Assessment Rubric

Name of Student _____

Skill (points awarded)	Consistently (3)	Sometimes (2)	Rarely (1)	Points
Listened carefully during teaching and while directions were being explained				
Imaginatively engaged with the material through journal				
Completed assignments (book report page, biography page, punctuation pages) in full				
Published written pieces with care				
Correctly used periods, question marks, and exclamation points				
Correctly used commas in a series or list				
Understood informational book well enough to illustrate what was read or answer questions correctly				
Participated in whole group discussions				
Able to work independently in a timely manner				
Contributed to small group work				

Total: _____

Comments (include punctuation rules with which the student might need extra help): _____

_____

_____

_____

_____

0-7682-3891-9 *Lightning Lessons: Nonfiction*

? Question Mark

A question mark ends a sentence that asks a question.

Was your brother the referee at your soccer game?

, Comma

1. A comma follows each item in a series except for the last item.

My baseball coach asked me to bring my glove, shoes, and a snack to

Punctuat

Period

1. A period is used at the end of a sentence that is a statement or command.

   Tennis is my favorite sport.

2. A period is used after abbreviations and initials.

   J.T. plays tennis every weekend at Smith School on Avery Rd.

Exclamation Mark